Introductio

1

Whilst working on this project, my Granny, Kathleen Cunningham, lost her long (17 years) battle with cancer; she passed away on 23rd October 2008 peacefully at home with her family at her side. She was a truly inspirational person who taught me to believe in myself and others, which can be particularly hard when you're looked upon as "them Travellers" or "the Gypsies". She taught me to be proud of who I am, as indeed she was, and to celebrate and not hide the fact that I am a Romany Gypsy. She even researched our family trees, which date back to the 1800's. This is why I think it is important to celebrate our culture and heritage. Other cultures do this, so why not Gypsies and Travellers?

When I was first approached to do this project I was a bit apprehensive. What if no one sent in pictures? What if no one ran events? Or went to events? All this anxiety was soon dispelled after a day on the phone and Internet! I also wanted Travellers themselves to contribute to the book, not just the services and organisations working with them and to do this proved difficult so I decided to run a photo competition with five winners receiving a digital camera. I promoted this through the Traveller Education Services, the Gypsy, Roma and Traveller History Month (GRTHM) website and the Travellers Times and the response was amazing. I sent out over 100 disposable cameras across the country and over half of them were returned. Altogether over 1000 pictures were entered into the competition! We held a pre-judging event with Jake Bowers (Romany Journalist) and Sandra Gregory (daughter of the late Eli Frankham) among the judges. The final 10 pictures were then chosen and put in the winter 2008 issue of Traveller Times for the public to text vote their winners. This was a very important part of the project for me because it involved the whole community. The five winners' pictures are included in this book along with their views on why they entered the competition. An exhibition of all the photographs entered is planned for future Gypsy, Roma and Traveller History Months.

I no longer live in a trailer or travel from place to place but if you come into my home the culture is there. Speak to me and the language is there.

From doing this project I have been in contact with Gypsy, Romany & Irish Travellers throughout the country and many services and organisations that support and work with them. If it wasn't for them and their hard work and passion none of this would have happened. And if by doing this publication we change the views of just one person then it will have been worth it.

Rose Wilson

Foreword

Gypsy, Roma and Traveller History Month – June 2008

We are fortunate that a number of ideas came together in 2007 which allowed for the preparations to be made for the first ever Gypsy, Roma and Traveller History Month (GRTHM). The idea came from a number of sources coincidentally, but in particular, acknowledgement should be given to Mr Rocky Deans of the Brent Traveller Education Support Service who had pioneered this work over a number of years, and Mr Peter Saunders of the Leeds Gypsy Roma Traveller Achievement Service who suggested the idea to the Department in the autumn of that year.

Lord Andrew Adonis, the then Minister at the Department for Children, Schools and Families, endorsed this first GRTHM despite the ubiquitous and unjust low public esteem awarded to Gypsy, Roma and Traveller communities across Europe. An increasing number of sensible and unprejudiced people are aware of the richness that Gypsy, Roma and Traveller communities bring to our society through their many and varied academic, creative and artistic skills and achievements. The typical racist nature of reporting in some of the media on the life and work of these marginalised communities only serves to continue to obscure and distort the reality of the enormous contribution they have made to British society over many centuries.

This wonderful book of photographs provides a telling story of the many and varied events that took place up and down the country during the month of June in 2008. The publication has by necessity had to be very selective in terms of the final shortlist of photographs chosen for inclusion. I am sure that the editor, Rose Wilson, and her colleagues within the Cambridgeshire Race Equality and Diversity Service, had an extremely difficult task in the sorting and selection process. Apart from thanking and congratulating all the hundreds of experienced and budding photographers who sent in their photographs, I am sure that we should also congratulate the editorial team and their advisors for the excellent product that has resulted. We must all be indebted to all of them for this memorable historic archive which will be treasured by so many for so long.

I am always struck by the strange ironies of life. The history of the United Kingdom has nothing proud to boast when it comes to the treatment of these minority communities. Indeed, there is a shameful history of racist persecution, prejudice and discrimination. David Mayall in his book "English Gypsies and State Policies", graphically sums up this national past by saying, "In the history of Gypsies there have been numerous instances of public power – the official, legalised authority of the state – being used to specifically persecute this minority group. General surveys chronicle the story of enforced slavery, deportation, death penalties and attempted genocide."

What an irony it was then when the winners of the national GRTHM Poster Competition were invited to the House of Lords to receive their prizes from their Lordships, Eric Avebury and Andrew Adonis. So at the heart of government in the Houses of Parliament, there was a welcome and clear message that the significant contribution of these communities over time was now to be acknowledged and respected and that the discrimination and persecution should come to an end.

We are beautifully reminded of these historic events in this marvellous compilation of photographs.

Arthur Ivatts OBE

Welcome

I am delighted to provide the foreword for this impressive photographic record of the first national Gypsy, Roma and Traveller History Month.

This set of photographs will offer a permanent record to remember the many interesting and celebratory events which took place during June 2008. It will also raise awareness and allow schools to explore the history, culture and language of these communities. These topics are not usually included in the curriculum for all pupils, but resources like this will help change that situation. With this resource, teachers can challenge myths, tackle prejudice and be in a position to offer a balanced debate about the issues. It offers an opportunity to celebrate the richness that Gypsy, Roma and Traveller communities bring to our society through their many and varied academic and artistic achievements.

Those involved in pulling together and selecting all the photographs to produce such an eye-catching publication should be congratulated. The photographs have captured the spirit of so many different occasions within the inaugural History Month.

Many of the events captured were initiated and supported by local authority Traveller Education Support Services and hundreds of schools. Congratulations to those who contributed so much to making the History Month such a resounding success, especially to the children and their families for participating with such enthusiasm and confidence during this truly historic occasion.

Sarah McCarthy-Fry MP
Parliamentary Undersecretary of State for Schools and Learners

6 Appleby

Education on the Hoof at Appleby Fair is an annual event run by ACERT, the Advisory Council for the Education of Romanies and other Travellers.

This photograph shows children at Appleby enjoying a reading by Pippa Goodhart of "Toffee and Pie", her recently published book whose main character is a Traveller boy.

Barnsley

Rayner Morrison, who is a proud Barnsley born and bred Gypsy and one of the first Gypsy women to become a health trainer working for the Barnsley Primary Care Trust.

8 Bedfordshire

Pictured are students **Scarlet & Kenny-Joe** who helped advisory teachers Wendy McGinty & Lynn Stuart to prepare a library display illustrating the history and culture of Gypsy, Roma and Traveller communities.

Bulgaria

June 3-4

More than 700 children participated in the Fifth Children's Roma **Open Heart Festival** at Veliko Turnovo in Bulgaria. Many well-known Roma activists were guests at the Festival.

Cambridgeshire

Kelly Bath from St Neots in Cambridgeshire, receiving her East of England Outstanding Adult Learner of the year Award presented by Susie Fowler-Watt from BBC Look East at the Regional Awards ceremony.

Cardiff

Dr Brian Gibbon, Minister for Social Justice and Local Government, at the launch of the Save the Children **"Travelling Ahead"** DVD, produced with financial assistance from the Welsh Assembly Government. The event was held at the Cardiff Traveller Education Service's Open Day at the Shirenewton Site.

12 Cardiff

Clarice Evans from Cardiff in Wales entered the Gypsy, Roma and Traveller History Month Photograph Competition and was one of the five winners.

> " I thought it would be good to enter the competition because I like taking photos. I like taking pictures of my pets and my family. "
> **Clarice Evans**

Cardiff

Julie Ann McCann from Cardiff in Wales entered the Gypsy, Roma and Traveller History Month photograph competition and was one of the five winners.

" I entered the competition because I like taking photographs of my family, friends and pets. I love taking photographs of weddings, parties and when we go on holidays so I thought it would be good to enter. "
Julie-Anne McCann

Cornwall

The **St. Day Gypsy and Traveller Women's Group** held a showcase day for their films made as part of their Penpal DVD project. A group of young Gypsy and Traveller women from Cornwall linked up with a similar group in Romania.

The project is run jointly by TravellerSpace, a project supporting Gypsies & Travellers in Cornwall, and Barbara Santi, a local filmmaker.

Derbyshire

A photograph entered in the Gypsy, Roma
and Traveller History Month competition

It was taken by **John Kelly** from Derbyshire.

16 Doncaster

A **Storytelling and Literary Evening** was
held on 5th June 2008 at the Ukrainian Club
in Doncaster with writers Louise Doughty
and Richard O'Neill.

East Riding

The **Tree Planting Ceremony** held at Cottingham High School was attended by Arthur Ivatts and several members of the East Riding of Yorkshire Council, including the Chair of the Council, Bryan Pearson, who helped with the planting of the tree, along with Traveller pupils, members of staff, and guests from other agencies.

18 Ely

"The Lady in Red" tug boat owned by the McNaughton family and moored at Ely in Cambridgeshire during June 2008.

Epsom

Here we see families pulled on the Epsom Downs and one of the many china stalls on the market for the **Epsom Derby.**

These pictures were taken on "Ladies Day", Friday June 6.

Essex

Essex Traveller Education Service held an **Open Day** at their base, Alec Hunter Humanities College, in celebration of Gypsy, Roma and Traveller History Month on Wednesday 25 June 2008.

Great Yarmouth

This photograph taken by **Patrick Hoyland** from Great Yarmouth, was a Gypsy Roma Traveller History Month photograph competition winner.

Lancaster

Joseph Doran, aged 4, won first prize in the pre-school category of the national poster competition.

As his family was at Appleby Fair he was unable to attend the House of Lords to receive his prize. Instead the Mayor of Lancaster, Councillor Keith Budden, made the presentation in Lancaster. Joseph is pictured here with the Mayor and with Vicki Edwards of Kingsway Play Group in Heysham.

Leeds

Michael Collins on set during the performance of his play 'It's a Cultural Thing, Or is it?' performed during Gypsy, Roma and Traveller History Month Arts week at the Courthouse Theatre, Otley, Leeds on Thursday 28 June 2008.

This play, based on the life story of the Irish Traveller, Michael Collins, who is a professional writer and actor, sets about exploding the myths often created to stigmatise the Traveller communities.

Michael Collins outside the Courthouse Theatre with the 'sold out' sign for his new play *'Mobile'*.

24 Leeds *Romipen*

Romipen, the energetic dancers from Slovakia, in action. This was taken during the free Grand Finale Concert at Leeds Civic Hall on Saturday 28 June organised by the Roma Support Group in London and the Gypsy Roma Traveller Education Service in Leeds to mark the end of Gypsy, Roma and Traveller History Month.

Leeds *Romipen*

The Gypsy ensemble **Romipen** was created in April 2008 for the occasion of Gypsy, Roma and Traveller History Month in Leeds. Romipen's members are a group of Roma and non-Roma young musicians and dancers, who love Slovakian and Roma music and dance. The programme features original melodies and dances from the Roma villages of Slovakia, Hungary and Romania, which are all professionally arranged and feature the unique Roma style of playing on the violin, the viola, the double bass and the cimbalom. This photograph of Marek Konãek's Gypsy band was taken at their sell out concert performance at the Seven Theatre, Chapel Allerton in Leeds on Friday 27 June.

Leeds *Romani Rad*

The Grand Finale concert in Leeds Civic Hall.

Romani Rad is a group of Roma dancers and musicians from Poland. The exotic and colourful costumes are all designed and handmade by the Romani women.

The musicians are all highly skilled performers. They present a wide range of Gypsy songs and dances from different parts of Europe.

They performed in two concerts: to open Gypsy, Roma and Traveller History Month in London at Conway Hall on 4 June and to close it at the Civic Hall in Leeds on 28 June.

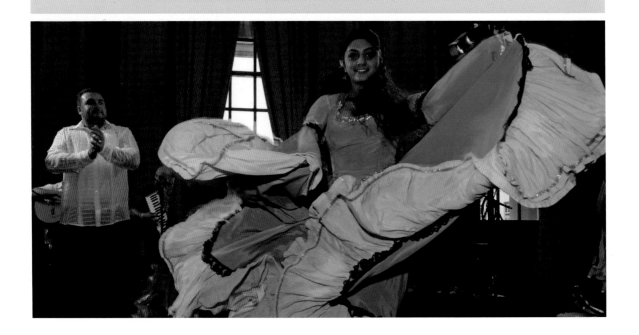

This photograph was taken at the opening of Ferdinand's first solo exhibition in England at **The Exhibition Space,** Central Library in Leeds on 16 June 2008.

Ferdinand is a Meckar Roma from Albania. Though now residing in London, Ferdinand has retained his Romani language and maintains strong links with his community.

Leeds
Jess Smith

Jess Smith,
Scottish Traveller, singer, storyteller and novelist, performing at the Seven Theatre.

Jess performed the world premiere of Richard O'Neill's 'The Hardest Word' monologue.
She received a standing ovation.

This powerful drama portrays the refusal of the Scottish government to apologise for its appalling treatment of the Scottish Traveller community.

Leeds
Sheila Stewart

Sheila Stewart MBE captivating her audience at the Seven Theatre in Leeds.

Sheila's family, the Stewarts of Blairgowrie, are famous all over the world for their rich cultural heritage of ballad singing, storytelling and music.

Sheila has also written two books, which are brilliant insights into the world of Scottish Travellers.

Leeds *Seven Concert*

Irish Traveller musicians, **William** and **Jimmy Dundon,** performing at the 'Seven' Concert in Chapel Allerton in Leeds.

The event featured music, stories, dramas and songs.

Lewisham

The **London Gypsy Orchestra,**
who came to perform at an event
held in Lewisham.

London

The Irish Traveller Movement's celebrations, **Pavee Ceilidh,** which took place in London on 26 and 27 June 2008. Here we see a traditional paper flower making activity for young people led by Breda Doran.

London
Brigid Corcoran

June 17

Brigid Corcoran performing at the London Gypsy and Traveller Unit's 10th anniversary celebrations. Brigid, a young Irish Traveller, has been described as country music's brightest rising star.

London

This historic photograph shows Lord Avebury, the great campaigner for the rights of Gypsies and Travellers in this country, presenting the **national poster prizes** to the winners during a moving celebration at the House of Lords on 2 June 2008 to open the first national Gypsy, Roma and Traveller History Month.

Back row: (left to right) Amie Scarratt, John Chadwick, Kayleigh Earle, Lord Avebury, Anne Miles, Lisa Sweeney **Front row: (left to right)** Savannah Doran, Elijah Lee, Felix Hanrahan, Ann Marie Eastwood and Jonathan Georgiades.

Middlesex

Bell Farm Christian Centre hosted an exhibition called
Passing Places. The exhibition was lent by Hertford
Museum and tells the history of the Travelling Community.

Children from local schools visited the centre, as well as
people from the Travelling community, the Over Sixty club
and countless others.

Newham

Following the relocation of the Newham Traveller site to make way for the Olympic Games, Lisa Smith, a resident on the site, suggested an **Open Day.** She opened her trailer to children from the local schools, along with their parents and teachers.

Young Travellers from across Norfolk worked with artist **Karl Foster** to explore their cultural heritage through the arts. This was part of a Norfolk County Council Children's Services Arts Partnership project with the Traveller Education Service and Gressenhall Museum of Rural Life.

"April's Horse" was designed by young Traveller April and made into a life-size piece of public art by the artist Karl Foster.

38 Norfolk

Lily Sheridan from Norfolk entered the Gypsy, Roma and Traveller, History Month photograph competition and was the overall winner.

Her picture was chosen out of thousands of photographs through a text vote run in Traveller Times magazine.

> " I am proud to be a Traveller and I love taking photos of how we really live! "
> **Lily Sheridan**

St Austell

An **Open Day** held at the Service base for Equality
& Diversity for Children's Services in St Austell, Cornwall.

A yurt was put up to hold art workshops, a display of the
history and heritage of Gypsies and Travellers, DVDs and
music and a graffiti wall. Everyone shared a picnic!!

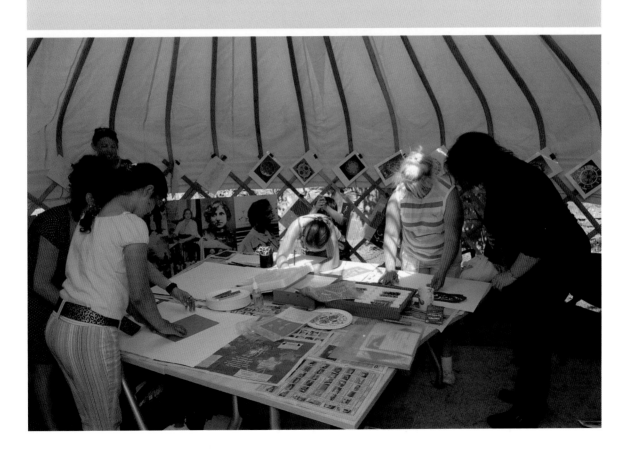

Surrey

Janet Keet Black of the Romany and Traveller Family History Society put together this exhibition about Queen Victoria's rat catcher, Matthias Cooper, who was a Romany. It was held at Bourne Hall Museum in Surrey on Saturday 28 June.

Tilford

Open days were held on 14 -15 June at The Rural Life Centre in Tilford at which **Nobby Melrose** opened up his Gypsy caravan and explained how he built it.

This superb replica Gypsy caravan was built by one of the support group members using only model plans. It took many hours of meticulous work and is complete inside as well as out.

Stinger Loveridge and **Sally Davies** pictured on 10 June at their homes on Wentworth Caravan Site near Cambridge.

Wisbech

Romany poet and author **Kathleen E. Cunningham** at the book signing for "The Great Romany Showman", based on the travels of her grandfather, Esau Carman.

The signing was held in the Market Place of Wisbech town centre, Cambridgeshire in June 2008.

44 Wisbech

Suzanna Hardwick from Wisbech in Cambridgeshire entered the Gypsy, Roma and Traveller History Month Photograph Competition and was one of the five winners.

> " I took photos of the old cars, trailers & lorry to show today's generation how the older Gypsies used to live. "
> **Suzanna Hardwick**

Woking

Pictured are **Gary Brazil** and the Epsom mayor.

Worcestershire

Pictured here is Joanne Clee at **Hartlebury Castle Museum,** where the regional celebration day for Gypsy, Roma and Traveller History Month took place on June 15. Many families from across the region attended and had a fantastic time.

The Kushti project is a family learning project for Gypsy families based at Landywood Children's Centre and many of the families went to Hartlebury Castle Museum on the day.

Index and photograph credits